MORELS :

TRUE OR FALSE

The Essential Field Guide
and More

MORELS:
TRUE OR FALSE

The Essential Field Guide
And More

Larry Lonik

R K T PUBLISHING

Hazel Park, MI 48030

MORELS: TRUE OR FALSE
The Essential Field Guide and More

First Edition, First Printing (1999)
Copyright © 1999 by Larry Lonik
ISBN : 0931715-04-0

Visit our website **www.morelheaven.com** for more information about books and other products, photos & current information, Lonik's appearances, special events and more....

Every effort has been made to ensure that all information, including images and opinions, is accurate and current. However, the author and publisher cannot accept any responsibility for loss, injury, illness or inconvenience, however caused, related to the content of this book.

R K T PUBLISHING

HAZEL PARK, MI 48030

Dedication

There are people in this world who give more than they receive,
who share and advise and encourage,
and ask nothing in return;
who protect, who challenge, who quietly exemplify
the best that human beings can be.
I have been privileged to have known some of these exceptional people.
They have directly influenced my life's work.
Though they have passed on to the next world,
their spirit lives, and because of them our world is a better place.
This book is dedicated to
Herb Cedarquist, Dr. Ray Davis, Claude Hawkins,
Harley Selling and Vonnie Howard

Table of Contents

Preface

Nearly every source of information I've encountered about morel mushrooms, over the last 30 years, has contained inaccuracies, some
of which could be confusing if not dangerous. This book addresses this
issue, head-on, in two ways: firstly, as a simple-to-use current field guide
with color photos of the types of morels, in their natural habitat and cross-
sectioned; and secondly, with the latest advice and information related to
frequently- and not-so-frequently-asked questions about morels, the expert answers to which can help make the morelling experience more effective and enjoyable for the novice, the seasoned "hunter" and the cook.

Morels are still the easiest to identify and safest to pick and eat of
all wild mushrooms, but the (certainly unintentional) just plain bad information continues to pile up. I've seen a gourmet food magazine that
showed a picture of a false morel and described it as a white (true) morel
(*Morchella esculenta*). Many articles claim that false morels are poisonous. The director of the Chamber of Commerce of a city that sponsors a
major mushroom festival regularly stated that the *Verpa bohemica* (a
false morel) is poisonous, but they are counted as "good" morels in their
picking contests! If you look in the mushroom field guides over the years,
you'll likely find a variety of descriptions and precautions that, when
compared guide-to-guide, don't agree. The examples go on and on....

The information that's put into the field guides is good and well
intentioned. When the books attempt to cover thousands of species that
have on-going related research, reports and updates, it is literally impossible to be 100% correct. As an example, I recently perused a new (1998)
field guide from a very well known, large publishing house. Within 15
minutes I found 4 mistakes. Other mushroom books and articles list up
to 20 different types of true morels and 50 false morels. No wonder

there's such confusion! It's not that these publications are sloppy or outdated. It's simply that the task is formidable. On the other hand, I study and write about morels—from a variety of perspectives (science, research, decades of outdoor experience, culinary, cultivation, etc.), and only morels.

Morels are an ideal "first mushroom". Armed with basic knowledge of when to look, where to look and what you're looking for, you can be successful. The more you learn, the better the chances you will be more effective. Pre-planning before the season is an excellent way to improve your odds. There is exercise involved. It can be strenuous or leisurely, but the activity is adaptable to many lifestyles and capabilities. Be forewarned and be ready.

Resources are available…mushroom clubs and organizations, festivals, magazines, books, videos, the World Wide Web. All can enhance this wonder-filled outdoor experience.

In addition to the color field guide images and general text, is a section called "Ask the Tree". It's designed to enlighten the reader about specific information related to morel hunting, cooking, preservation, reconstituting, growing attempts (indoors and outdoors), etc. Many misconceptions, problems (like ruined morels), and questions about increasing yields or "seeding" areas have prompted me to create this section this way. It can be a fine-tuning for the experienced morel fan or a primer of sorts for the new to the fold.

The questions have originated from the hundreds of seminars I've conducted over the years and thousands of interviews and contacts with morel enthusiasts, chefs, scientists, writers, photographers, radio and television people, and dogs. Many people (and one dog I know of) think of themselves as morel experts (10 million people hunt morels in North America every Spring. It's estimated that as many as 4 million get "skunked"), but we can all learn a thing or two. Many of us have had our share of good and bad luck (not always luck), spoiled mushrooms, unusual sightings, rumors, suggestions and stories. It's the compilation of expert advice from a multitude of sources that make "Ask the Tree" valuable to anyone interested in morels.

A third goal, hopefully inherent in the style and content of this book, is to be interesting, informative and stimulating—just like the entire morel experience should be. Please enjoy the book and the outdoors.

So many people have contributed to the effort that has resulted in the books of this series. It's impossible to thank them all without missing some. The mushroom cap is eternally tipped to all, including: Mom and Dad, Cathy, Barry and Lara, Crimson and King, Mike Mikula, Jim Tuman, Jim Utley, The Mr. Mushroom gang, Lex and Sherry Maples, Lina and Rich Blaut, Chris Carl (webmaster), the Detroit Entrepreneurial Institute family, Leonard and the Peases, Vicky and Tom Nauman and family, Brian Bishop, artist Lesley Pritchard, Hannelore Lebrecht, Tom Licavoli, photographer Taylor F. Lockwood, Ron and Deb at the Trail of Tears Lodge, Charlie and Linda Irons, Bill and Pam Snow, Ted and Jane Kowalewski, Susan Sparks, Susan Turcotte, Boyne City, Bookworld, Gilliland and Gary Espy, the Graphics Factory, Chris and Deana Williams, Sam Kosc, White-Not-White, Ed and Mary Ann Lawrence and thousands more....

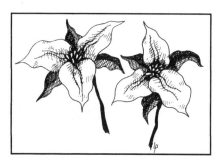

Trillium

NOTE: The sketches of flowers dispersed throughout this book are renditions of wildflowers commonly found at the time of year when morels appear, just another factor that makes the Spring-walk-in-the-woods experience so enjoyable.

Introduction

"What time is it?"

"Six thirty. As they say on Monty Python's Flying Circus, "No time to lose."

Stash and Doug immediately rang in, repeating "No time to lose."

All three then took turns for the next few minutes saying the phrase "No time to lose", changing the emphasis from word to word, altering the pace as if there were a prize for the most different ways one could utter those same four words. At times squawked like parrots, then sung like words to a tango. Then sobbed. Then pronounced like it was addressed to the Frenchman: "No time, Toulouse." It was getting very "Stooge"-like. And there were three of them. One named Larry. The (very) early signs of a crazy, and quite likely fun-filled, day were unfolding....

"What's the plan?"

Larry answered quickly so they wouldn't all start repeating "What's the plan?"

"Well, it's Sunday. That sucks. All the in-bred locals will be in the woods 'cause even the ones not on welfare won't be workin' today. Church will delay some. Then we got two hundred thousand trunk-slammin' fudgies up from the city for the weekend. Boys, we got competition."

"The Great Mushroom Hunt continues, against all odds. What do we have so far—three?"

"Yeah, Tree's got two. Me one. Doug's still a virgin."

"Well, it's a little tough to see in a monsoon. And I'm only two mushrooms behind the leader anyway. Why was Tree the leader again? We're doin' so well...."

"He's got experience, or so he says. Well at least it stopped raining. What's our odds today?

"Hey—wait a minute. Are *we* trunk-slammin' fudgies?"

"Well, we *are* up from the city. But I've got no plans to buy fudge or slam trunks...."

"Fudge doesn't sound too bad...."

"It's six thirty in the morning!"

"Gentlemen, please. Now, the ground cover looks good. A bit of green through the leaves. Trilliums are out—at their peak. It would've been nice if the sun could have bleached the leaves, like usual for this time of year. Since we're mostly looking for blacks, it makes it tougher to see that outline when the leaves are dark from being wet. No contrast. But...temperature—cooler than I'd like. Only 60 today. Water—no problem there. Rained 2 straight days. It'll probably start to dry up late morning. That's good and bad. May be the best pickin's going to be Tuesday and Wednesday. Sometimes when it's cool it takes a while for the rain to work it's magic."

"We'll be back in the office."

"Might be good days to call in sick. Say, Doug, you don't look well. I think you should take a few days off...."

"That's mostly 'cause I haven't been dry or warm since Friday when we got here."

"Or maybe it's the gasoline-flavored hotdogs we had for dinner...."

"Maybe Mr. Coleman's got our coffee water ready. Today's a new day. The last day of the Great Mushroom Hunt. And, hey, it's not raining. Maybe even see some sun later."

"Maybe see some morels?"

"We should see *something*. It's the heart of the season. That's why there's going to be cars along every dirt trail and road for hundreds of miles. Plus there's 3 mushroom festivals this weekend. More reasons why we've got to get started early. By noon most decent spots within a short walk from a car will have had visitors."

"Mother's Day usually good?"

"Depends. I've seen seasons end by Mother's Day. Others didn't start till after."

"How 'bout this year?"

"Well, we're still looking for blacks, though I think it's toward the end of the black season. They should be bigger—easier to spot. Slightly higher temperatures. A little more humidity. Maybe some small whites. This last rain should bring a whole new batch of big blacks and smaller whites. The rain probably washed a lot away too. The moisture content of a morel can be as high as 95% so a steady long drizzle can break them down."

"So that's why we've been out in the rain slippin' and slidin' on muddy leaf-covered hills?"

"One of the reasons. Plus we're nuts."

"So where to?"

"Five Corners first. Beat the crowd, if possible. Last year people camped right in the woods."

"That ain't fair. Why didn't we think of that?"

"All's fair in love and war. I'm just not sure which this is…. Anyway,

Columbine

we'll try there. Good area. Way too accessible. Bunches of people know about Five Corners—locals and fudgies."

"What's the deal on the Indiana and Ohio license plates? They like fudge that much?"

"Actually, they've already picked in their own states. Now they come to Michigan at the same time the mushrooms arrive. Morels appear 100 miles further north each week. There's more woods and public land here. And now there's some bucks in it. Heavy bread, man.. The root of all evil. And another reason to get started."

"Know your competition."

"But what does the competition know about the Great Mushroom Hunters?"

"I'm sure they're worried. I would be too. In fact I am."

"Yeah, we've taken three morels out of the world supply so far. We're definitely a threat."

(A coffee toast.)

"After Five Corners, Three Sisters. It's south. Easy access again. Not as well-known. Hasn't been a good spot in the last few years, but I slayed 'em there a while back. It's part of the Valley of Roads complex that has some other excellent spots—if they're bitin'. We could stay there all day, easy. Lunar Landscapes One and Two, Deer Skull Trail, Zebra Tree. Took several years to map out the good spots. You can really get lost too. I did. Slept under a pine tree in a cold rain one night. Got down to some basic survival. Hypothermia. Easy to get lost when it's overcast and getting late. Had a grocery sack full of black morels though. Sack was fallin' apart from the rain. Had to carry it like a baby. Now I use mesh bags (we all got to learn), and I carry a compass and a whistle."

"There's a couple of roads that cut right through the woods. You can hunt from the car. It's deluxe. Whenever you see one, you just hop out and check the area. Remember, when you find one there's usually more."

"Except in The Great Mushroom Hunt."

"Three Sisters is three black ash trees growing together near the road. If it's decent we'll stay a while. Maybe come back. But we have to get to One-Eye's by 9:30. It's the most predictable place for blacks I know of. Always something there, and depending on what, where and how many, I can evaluate how the season is progressing. There's an open area near the road that produces small blacks first. Then they go deeper into the woods as the season goes on, getting more and larger. It's my "indicator" spot. Been going there over 15 years. Even though the best areas are right along the road, I always park further up the trail and circle back so no one finds the spot. There's at least one local guy who comes out every Sunday after church, about 11:00. So we want to be gone by then."

"Where's One-Eye's?"

"About sixty miles south of Three Sisters. Mushroom hunting sometimes means travel. Gotta go where the mushrooms are. My indicator spot, One-Eye's—named after a an old one-eyed friend who lived nearby, will tell us where to go after that. In the afternoon we'll probably have to go "remote". Either we park and walk deep into a woods or we drive where no one else is stupid enough to drive. I've got some ideas and experience along those lines also."

"I bet you do. Sometimes the old warm office doesn't sound so bad...."

"You gonna call your Mom?"

"I haven't seen my Mom on Mother's Day since I graduated from high school. I'm always in the woods on weekends in May. I *think* she understands...."

"She probably appreciates it—no maniac to ruin her day."

"I always call her—usually in the evening. I do get to think about a lot of things—including her—in the woods. We'll call—later."

(Another coffee toast) "To our mothers."

"To all the mothers."

"Time to drink up and saddle up, lads. Sun'll be comin' up soon."

The chorus sings, "No time to lose."

This, only-slightly-altered tale, is oddly typical of a real mushroom outing. The weather. The strategy. The pet names for favorite spots. The sharing of knowledge and experience. Adversity. Comradeship. Fun. It's addictive.

Since 1955 (when I was 6 years old), I've never missed a Spring "treasure hunt." Most years my harvest averages 100 pounds. There were a couple of lean seasons when I found less than a dozen—total! But those were Springs when my time was limited and the weather was inhospitable. It happens. There also have been times when the "Bonus" light went on—80 pounds in one afternoon, for example—morels carpeted a series of five low rolling hills. I've had a couple of 40 pound days also, but on a good day I'll walk 15 miles and collect 10 pounds of morels.

My annual goal is to pick 100 pounds. I eat, give away or do cooking demonstrations and shows with 50 pounds. The other half I dry, weigh out 2 ounces, put that amount into a small paper sack (like a child's lunch bag), fold it over, tape it shut, then toss it under my bed. Then, any time in Summer, Fall or Winter, I can hang my head over the side of my bed and count the bags. If I start off with 50 bags I can have one pound of morels every week to get me back to the next morel season. (The 2 ounces, when re-hydrated, become a full pound, an 8:1 ratio). I don't like being without morels.

By the way, there is no intention to offend any of the previously-mentioned groups, including in-breds, fudge eaters, trunk slammers, mothers, office workers, people with one eye, churchgoers, or the Three Stooges. It would be difficult to offend Monty Python.

Mayapple

PART ONE: MOREL MUSHROOMS

What Are They?

10 million North Americans look for morels every year.
The fun and excitement of an Easter Egg Hunt coupled with the unique

*These morels were all found in the same location within one hour.
The long one is a semi-libera, then clockwise: white morel, black morel,
Gyromitra, white morel, and Helvella.*

steak-like flavor and texture (with no calories) lure people of all ages
and backgrounds into remote fields and forests in search of this delight-
ful and elusive prize. On the whole, it's a quiet group. Though
there are festivals and clubs, magazines and books, morellers look for
and/or have favorite hunting spots. No special equipment or license is
required (though being considered in some cases) and productive locations are closely guarded secrets. The "reclusive" characteristic of morels is often shared by morel hunters.

Understanding what morels are, when and where they're found,
and identifying resources for the ever-expanding body of knowledge related to morels, can help the novice and the pro become more effective
in their efforts.

Mushrooms are fungi (the plural of fungus). Fungi are organisms that grow and fruit like most plants, but differ in the fact that they
do not have roots, leaves, stems, flowers, seeds, or chlorophyll. Fungi
include mold and crusts. The larger fungi are commonly known, generally, as mushrooms. They reproduce by single-celled spores.

Black morels drying in the sun. The white powder is spore.

The two major divisions of mushrooms are basidiomycetes (club fungi) and ascomycetes (sac fungi). Most of what we call "mushrooms" are basidiomycetes. Morels, and truffles, are ascomycetes. What we pick in the woods is the fruit of the organism, which is stimulated to appear in the Springtime (though the season varies in North America from February to August, depending on location, and has opposite seasonal appearances in the Southern Hemisphere). The technical details of the variations, life cycles, toxins, etc. are available from many sources. This book is meant to be a *practical* field guide—for the millions of morel enthusiasts who desire to be more effective in their efforts with the highest degree of comfort and safety possible. Morels continue to be studied, sought after and written about. Attempts to grow them also add to the bank of knowledge, as does information related to wild harvests around the globe.

Fungi simply exist to break down decaying material into reusable substances. Because of their nature most fungi contain some type of toxin. These toxins, when ingested by a human being, can cause allergic reactions, even death. Reliable and current information is critical to safely enjoying mushrooms. Morels are the easiest to identify and safest to pick and eat, but, even with morels, one needs to be cautious. Additionally, much of the material available is incomplete, outdated or inaccurate.

The morel organism can be thought of as similar to an apple tree with roots, fruit, leaves, a trunk and branches. The apple tree grows fruit not to feed us humans, but to grow more apple trees—survival. Though we pick the "mushroom" or "fruit", the entire organism exists underground—a network of storage and retrieval systems with amazing intelligence and adaptability.

Giant morel (Morchella crassipes).

Mushrooms reproduce from spore. In the case of morels, the cap of the mushroom contains 250,000 to 500,000 spores (asci). The morel (fruit) tries to maximize the number and quality of its spore to release into the atmosphere. The spore falls on the ground, germinates and grows hyphae and mycelium, a network of thin, spiderweb-like fibers similar to roots that grow downward to a level that the organism senses is safe and practical. At that level (which in many situations is just below the frost line), the hyphae begin pulling nutrients through its network to store underground. The nutrients are from decaying leaves, branches, grass, etc. The nutrient warehouse, known as "sclerotia", is a solid mass that can vary in size, but generally can be thought to be about the size of a base-ball. The sclerotia is insulated from frost and freeze in most cases, but the hyphae to the surface cannot survive colder temperatures. In Spring the sclerotia sends new tendrils (hyphae) to the surface, this time for the purpose of reproduction. At some point the decision is made to push out the fruit, which is connected to the mycelial mat at the surface as well as the sclerotial mass below. 10 million North Americans hunt for this fruit.

Many scientific principles are at work here, some certainly not understood completely and under study. The spore must locate a com-patible strain, but the preferences, strengths and other genetic consider-ations are questionable. How long does it take for sclerotia to mature to the point it regularly bears a substantial amount of fruit? What factors affect the organism at that time? Weather? Age? Nutrient requirements? In the comparison to the apple tree, how big/how old does the tree need to be before it bears some apples, then a full crop? Some recent studies suggest morels have a five-year cycle.

Photo By Taylor F. Lockwood

A burn-over morel, common in the Pacific Northwest.

Does the organism use the same fruiting tendrils to collect nutrients? What are the roles of surface and ground water? Trauma (flood, fire, disturbing substrate) stimulates growth and increases yields. What are the cyclical effects of traumatized areas? Research has gone on for decades, and continues….

Morels can be divided into two types: true morels and false morels. Some call the true "morels" and the false "lorchels". For the most part, we'll use true and false as the basic categories. True morels have 1) pitted caps, 2) hollow stems, and 3) the bottom of the cap meets the top of the stem. False morels have 1) wavy indented caps, 2) a cotton-like substance in the stem, and 3) the cap hangs like a bell or a skirt. There are some exceptions, of course, but if you can check off three yeses to the description above, you're, as they say, "good to go."

A lovely meal featuring 3 morel dishes: cream of morel soup, Chateau Briand with a morel glaze, and a king crab and morel stir-fry. The exquisite flavor can be enjoyed at the campsite as well as white tablecloth restaurants.

Nutrients for the morel organism are stored in a "warehouse" under the ground. It is called "sclerotia" (skla-ro-sha) and is pictured here in a laboratory. In nature about the size of a potato, it sends its tendrils (hyphae) to the surface for nutrients and to produce fruit. The fruit is what millions of people hunt for. The photo below is a morel growing in a laboratory. Note the white "mycelia" on the dirt. In nature the mycelia will be spread in a "mat" throughout the top layer of soil.

There are 7 kinds of morels that are most common (true and false combined). These seven will be pictured (in their home habitat and cut in half) and detailed:

1. Black Morel (true) – M. Angusticeps
2. White Morel (true) — M.Esculenta
3. Giant Morel (true) — M. Crassipes
4. Half-free Morel (true) – M. Semilibera
5. Skirt-cap Morel (false) — Verpa
6. Beefsteak Morel (false) – Gyromitra
7. Saddle Morel (false) – Helvella

There are variations, though slight. Some sources list, for example, Morchella conica, M. elata and the burn-over morels in addition to M. angusticeps (black morel). I classify them all as black morels, for 2 basic reasons: 1) they are the first of the "true" variety to appear, and 2) it's simple and practical.

What I call "white" morels include "grays", "yellows" and Morchella deliciosa, which can have an almost "albino"-like appearance. I call them "white morels" because they are next in succession to arrive, after the black morels. The giants come last.

Don't look for morels in November (in the US)! This real photo from my backyard is from an experiment related to stimuli and vegetative stages of growth.

The Morel Season (approximately one month in any location)

first week	second week	third week	fourth week
True black morels		True white morels	
			True giant morels
	True half-free morels		
FalseVerpa			
	False Gyromitra		
False Helvella			

The progression of warming temperatures and increasing humidity (along with other specific weather conditions) affects the fruiting/availability cycles. For example, as the "black season" ebbs, smaller white morels can be found in the same areas. The stipe (stem) walls of the black morels become thinner than those of the previous week, and the mushrooms grow larger. One week later, only whites can be found. They, then, get larger as their season advances.

Lady's Slipper

A similar method is used to classify the false morels. The Verpa Bohemica has a cousin with a smooth cap (not pitted or wavy) often called a Verpa Conica. But the cap is "loose" and the stem usually contains the same "cotton" as the Bohemica does.

Around the world up to 50 varieties of morels have been listed. The basic 7 are described here. Remember that the general rule of identification always applies: If you're not sure, leave it alone.

Overall there are approximately 10,000 types of mushrooms in North America. 25 are edible and choice. 10 can kill you. The vast majority are just not palatable. Allergic reactions to eating mushrooms vary and can range from nausea and cramps to central nervous system attacks. One's first experience with any mushroom should involve ingesting a very small amount initially and waiting up to two hours before eating more. Individual tolerances also vary, and can change. Always be cautious and aware. As the mushroom field guide author and true gentleman, Dr. Alexander Smith, always concluded his presentations: "We don't know everything yet."

Dogwood

MORELS
Where Are They ?

Morels grow in every US state, every province of Canada, and most countries around the world. Ideal climates, for optimum yields, seem to lie in latitudinal belts which experience pronounced seasonal changes (north of the Mason-Dixon Line in the United States, for example). The Pacific Northwest is well known for a wide variety of mushrooms and the commercial wild harvesters collect well over a million pounds of morels every Spring. North American restaurant supply predominantly comes from this area. Tens of thousands of pickers roam the woods. The state of Washington has 10 mushroom clubs. The area's season, because of climate and elevations, can last three months or more. Ohio's season, on the other hand, averages three weeks in length. In Missouri, two weeks.

Morels grow outdoors, in season, in fields and forests. The variety of terrain (hardwoods in Minnesota, Douglas fir in the Rocky Mountains, tundra in Alaska, cottonwood and brambles in areas of the South) is extensive.

Internationally, morels are very popular in many parts of the world, but especially in Europe. As a country, Germany has the highest per capita consumption of mushrooms. France and Switzerland are not far behind. The Scandinavian countries traditionally have 25-30 types of mushrooms in their markets. The demand for mushrooms, including morels, is enormous. Commercially-harvested morels for the European market come from India, Pakistan and Turkey. Morocco, Peru, Nepal, Afghanistan, China, Russia and many, many other countries have commercial harvests as well. It's a crop, an income source to many. It's also an enjoyable, healthy, outdoor family activity with few financial strings. Knowing what to look for and when to look will help you hone in on the "where".

Spring Beauty

MORELS

When Do They Grow ?

In North America morels first appear in early February in areas of southern California, then they migrate north at the rate of about 100 miles per week, to Alaska and the Northwest Territories of Canada in late August. If you're standing still in mid-Michigan the wave of morels (first blacks, then whites, then giants) washes over you in the month of May.

The jet stream, elevations and weather conditions affect the onset of the morel season as well. The western (coastal) areas of Washington, for example, have considerably more rain than 200 miles inland. This simple characteristic dramatically alters the morel season and harvesting strategies between two areas essentially at the same latitude.

In the Southern Hemisphere the morel seasons begin late in the calendar year.

The best indicator may be temperature: the first string of days with average lows of 40-45 degrees Fahrenheit and 65-70 degree highs. This time can vary from year to year by a week or two (on the calendar), but, accordingly, so does the onset of the morel season.

There are other indicators: the stages of buds and leaves on tree branches, the amount of green growth pushing through the leafy ground cover, the mysterious increase of cars and trucks parked along two-rut trails in the middle of nowhere, and the beautiful array of wildflowers that adorn the woods specifically at this time of year. It can be helpful to observe and document the indicators at productive morel spots in your area, and look for those indicators each year.

MORELS:

Resources

There are a number of available resources that can be tapped to help enhance your morelling experience, whether your interest lies in mycology (science), mycophagy (eating), photography, taxonomy (classification), toxicology (poisonous effects), group activity, books, magazines, videos, memorabilia, and more.

For the first-timer I recommend the mushroom festivals, (especially) the mushroom clubs, or a guided hunt. The festivals will place you in the midst of mushroom enthusiasts, many of whom are novices. There usually are basic seminars, taste tests and picking contests. Contact your state Travel Bureau for festival dates and agendas.

Mushroom clubs are excellent vehicles to meet people who are knowledgeable, experienced and willing to share what they know. The groups have several forays from Spring to Fall, for a number of edible and choice wild mushrooms. They often have displays, dinners and special events. There are about 100 organizations across in North America. To find an organization in your area (or where you're headed), contact:

North American Mycological Association (NAMA)
Joe Miller, executive secretary
10 Lynn Brooke Place
Charleston, West Virginia 25312-9521
Phone (304) 744-1654
Email: joemiller@citynet.net

Mushroom, the Journal of Wild Mushrooming is a national quarterly magazine that covers a full range of information related to mushrooms. Contact at: Box 3156 Moscow, Idaho 83843.

There are some interesting sites on the World Wide Web if you have access to the Internet....

www.morelheaven.com hopefully will be the most comprehensive, interactive site for those interested in morels and other mushrooms. Latest findings, photos, art, quotes, Larry Lonik's tours and appearances, recipes, questions and answers, tips, stories, books & videos, Spore Boy mushroom bags, links to other sites and more.

So, you're not alone—unless you want to be alone. There are millions of morel (and other mushroom) enthusiasts on the planet. We can all do better, learn more, be more responsible and enjoy this wonderful activity that we are privileged to have available to us. Just do it.

Morchella Angusticeps BLACK MOREL
TRUE
GOOD

DETAILS: 2"-6" tall, earliest of the true morels. Hollow stem, tan to dark or gray cap. Also know as conica, elata, burn-over morel, narrow-capped morel, witch's cap, Johnny Jump-ups. Found in forests, burned over areas. Earthy aroma. Hearty, meaty flavor.

Hollow stem, attached to bottom of cap, cap is "pitted".

Morchella Angusticeps BLACK MOREL

TRUE

GOOD

Morchella Esculenta WHITE MOREL

TRUE

GOOD

DETAILS: 2"-8" tall, normally found after black morels, in forests, edges of fields, orchards and open areas. Hollow stem, blond, yellow, tan, gray or white in color. Generally rounder and meatier than blacks. Also known as deliciosa, "honeycombs", "grays", "yellows", "sponges" and "domes". Meaty flavor.

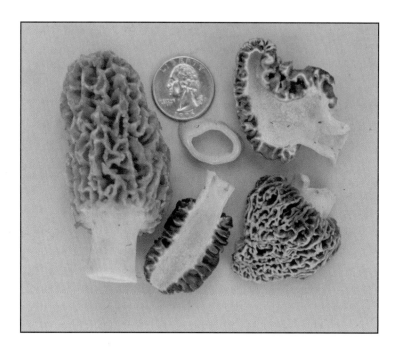

Hollow stem, attached to bottom of cap, pitted cap.

Morchella Esculenta WHITE MOREL

TRUE

GOOD

Morchella Crassipes   GIANT MOREL
TRUE

GOOD

DETAILS: 4"-12" tall, last of the true morels to appear. Hollow stem, tan, yellow or creamy in color. Found in forests, edges of fields and fencerows, orchards and grasses. Meaty flavor. Also known as "big foots" and thick-footed morels.

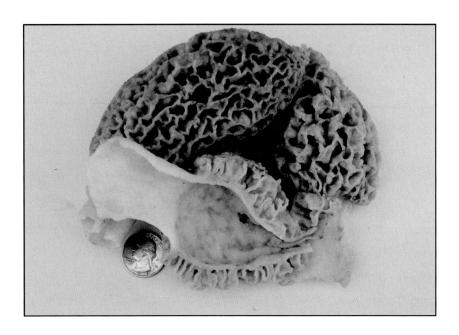

Hollow stem, attached to bottom of cap, pitted cap.

Morchella Crassipes **GIANT MOREL**

TRUE

GOOD

Morchella Semilibera   **HALF-CAP MOREL**

TRUE

GOOD

DETAILS: 2"-8" tall, usually appears same times as blacks, in forested areas. Hollow stem, attached midway in cap. Brown to black in color. Meaty flavor. Also known as "half-free" morel.

Note the hollow stem which clearly identifies this as a true morel. The stems are usually tall with thin walls, the caps smaller than the caps of black morels, which these resemble in coloring. Usually appear after the start of blacks.

Morchella Semilibera   HALF-CAP MOREL

TRUE

GOOD

SAVE THE MUSHROOMS!

Mushrooms are disappearing and you can help.

Spore Boy to the rescue.

The numbers of edible and choice wild mushrooms are decreasing at a faster rate than previously thought. Deforestation and the increased use of pesticides have been considered the culprits in this disappearing act and, indeed these two factors probably have been responsible for lower yields in areas where mushrooms are normally found. Many a morel fancier has reported treasured hot spots leveled in the name of development. Intermittent stories from around the world support the theory. But now, with the increased popularity of mushroom hunting and the commercial sector unleashing tens of thousands of income-seeking pickers into the woods and fields, a new nemesis, far more potentially devastating, is emerging. The methods of collection, particularly the vessels used to hold the precious booty, are preventing our beloved mushrooms from reproducing.

I've been studying mushrooms since 1970. Two factors, only recently come to light, reveal an emergency situation that has been neglected. Firstly, the type of harvest bag material has traditionally been paper or plastic. I've been guilty. For nearly 20 years I would stop at any grocery store for the optimistic "four paper bags, please." A collector in Missouri boasts in a home-made video about the 6 bread bags he filled that day--better than his previous high of 5 bread bags. Some people prefer wicker baskets. Tens of thousands of paid mushroom hunters in the Pacific Northwest are issued five-gallon empty plastic buckets to fill up as they roam the recently burned-over forests for morels. Hunters are going into more remote locations. Forests are deliberately being set afire to stimulate greater crops. In thousands of interviews with morel enthusiasts the vessel-of-choice related to me was primarily paper or plastic. They're cheap. They're easy to find. *But they're preventing spore from getting to the ground!* Nearly all of the morellers I've talked to tell me they used to find more mushrooms, a lot more mushrooms. Even taking into consideration that all mushroom hunters exaggerate, the trend has been obvious. The reason, though has not been clear--until now, and the status is worse than it appears!

Mushrooms reproduce by means of spore. The fruit of the morel organism (the mushroom we pick) contains hundreds of thousands of microscopic spores that are intended to return to the earth for their reproduction. With captured mushrooms in buckets and bags, by more and more pickers, this "re-seeding" is just not happening.

The knockout punch came more recently as I reviewed scientific evidence that seems to indicate that morel spore takes 5 years to create another mushroom. A spore hits the ground in the year 2000 and becomes a morel in 2005. We're in trouble if we don't act now! We're in trouble from the habits of the last five years as it stands. Fortunately there is a solution, and the long-term prospects are extremely promising, if we act now....

All mushroom hunters MUST use mesh bags when collecting mushrooms--at all times. This will allow spores to drop back to the forest floor as the picker walks--over a much greater area than the mushroom itself could have hoped to cover. Indeed, we can help Mother Nature as this method also mixes strains of spore, virtually ensuring compatibility. Walking in other areas with a mesh bag full of mushrooms can also seed *new* locations. Again, it takes years, but if one keeps going back....

Kids! Environmentalists! Outdoorspeople! Mushroomers! Naturalists! Legislators! We have been mushrooming incorrectly for decades, and we have years of decreased yields immediately ahead. But the trend can be reversed. We probably can't prevent urban sprawl, deforestation and pesticide use, but we can help seed the forests with mushroom spore, very much like the legendary Johnny Appleseed....

The Spore Boy mesh bag (logo above) was specifically designed for mushroom collection. It's soft and lightweight, yet sturdy, with beltloops, comfortable handles and a self-storing pouch--the result of years of input. It gently holds and aerates your harvest while maximizing the escape of spore. The bag retails for $8.00 with one dollar going to Mushrooms For Medicine, a non-profit organization developing natural remedies for arthritis and cancer. The bags are available from the **www.morelheaven.com** website and Morel Mania. Show that you know and you care. Join with Spore Boy and save the mushrooms!

PART TWO

"ASK THE TREE"

Expert Answers to Your Questions

Q: **How fast do morels grow?**

A: Most morels seem to literally "pop" out, quite often overnight. I
once came across a nice patch of black morels, averaging 5-6 inches
tall, just as the sun was setting into the leafless trees in the dis-
tance. As I picked I noticed that the stems were an iridescent pink,
not the usual white or cream color. Many of the morels were "bent
over". I'd seen on occasion where a twig or leaf had prevented a
morel from completely straightening up, and a few others bent for
no apparent reason, but never so many as this—maybe every fifth
or sixth morel was crooked. And I gradually noticed that my fingers and hands were getting very cold. I could see more morels in
the area, but it was getting dark. I picked as quickly as I could,
sensing the great fortune to find such a place and the frustration
that I was surely running out of visibility. I'd set my bag down to
mark a nice grouping, then my hat at another spot, then I piled

Wild Strawberry

morels to return for—all the while my hands were getting colder. They were nearly numb. I scrambled around, seeing more mushrooms nearby but realizing I would soon be unable to locate them and others that must certainly be nearby. As all light left I couldn't find the piles I had made. I didn't want to leave. I tried to think of ways to illuminate the forest: flashlights, headlights, setting fire to the woods, but I knew I was defeated for now.

But I still had tomorrow. I had to give an early morning lecture and then take a group of fifty on a guided mushroom hunt, but I could race the 90 miles to get back here by 11:00 am. I'd gas up tonight and be ready and drooling.

On the drive north to the cabin I'd be staying at I suddenly realized what I had been so fortunate to behold. I was watching morels growing! The bent morels were unfolding! They would straighten up in the night. The pink was from the freshness. The cold, I believe now, was from the underground moisture and nutrient warehouse (sclerotia) that was being fed upward through the mycelium ("root system"). The recently thawed soil was still very cold below ground level. It also hit me that these organisms were waiting for the sun to go down before they came out. The sun's rays would dry their "skin" and inhibit their growth. The survival instincts and adaptability astounded me. Another flush of great new respect for Mother Nature swept through me. What an exciting ride I had, with my bent, pink-stemmed mushrooms on the passenger seat, anticipating a big day tomorrow.

I did my chores and was back at the spot at 11:30. I walked the grounds in total shock—there were no mushrooms! No signs of another picker before me, and I know I hadn't been dreaming. In fact I don't believe I had slept. That night the temperature had fallen. The frost had quickly frozen the new mushrooms and, when the temperature rose, they melted like icecubes in a frying pan. Gone. Nothing. 15 hours earlier I had scrambled around the exact same spot, with cold hands, trying to figure out how to get more light. The fickle finger of fate. Even the mushrooms guessed wrong this time.

I've conducted many other experiments related to the rapidity of morel growth. One time I found a small black morel early in the season, put a quarter next to it and took a photo. I came back four consecutive days, at the same time of day, and took photos each time. The morel never grew but one day a morel twice its size had grown right in front of it.

I have seen photo sets of a morel growing gradually and I know people who leave morels to pick later. These instances usually involve cool, dry, shady conditions, but I have seen the evidence. I believe these are the exceptions.

Indoors, in controlled environments, morels do grow more slowly—10-14 days to reach peak size once the fundament has broken the surface. Many scientists over the years have told me that morels in the wild also grow slowly. Like politics and religion, it's not worth

Dogwood

arguing about. I have my reasons, millions of them, for my opinions...

Q: We used to find loads of morels around elm trees. Are certain trees good places to look?

A: Around elms used to be good places to look, and in many cases across the country, still are. Elms have been easy to spot. You looked for a bare trunk with slipping bark. Because of the Dutch elm disease many of these trees were dying and there was a nutritional surge from the root system. The morel organism had plenty of food to maximize its need to produce fruit. There seems to be less success near elms now leading me to believe the relationship was temporary. There are trends to look for white morels near black ash trees in northern latitudes. In other areas people look toward Douglas fir, apple or peach trees, poplar and cottonwood. There have been studies about symbiotic relationships, like the mutually beneficial tie between truffles and oak trees, but nothing conclusive has emerged concerning morels. The variety of places morels decide to appear is part of the mystique, challenge and fun.

Q: Does the organism die if you pull a mushroom up by its roots?

A: No. Think of the organism as being similar to an apple tree, only the tree is underground. Disturbing the "roots" is like pulling a small branch off the apple tree. The tree doesn't appreciate it much, but it won't kill the tree. The main reason to cut or pinch off the stem away from the roots is to keep the mushrooms clean.

Q: How come they're so rich?

A: Don't drown them in butter. If you choose to use butter as a sauté base select good butter and sauté at a high temperature. It will seal in the earthy, meaty taste.

Q: How do you get the dirt out?

A: Don't put it in! Morels come out of the ground clean. Most people
that complain about dirt and sand have not picked or cut the stems
cleanly and allowed some root dirt into their collection bag. Just a
small amount of grit can get caught in those tiny crevices and make
it difficult to wash out. Using a mesh collection bag will help allow any dirt to drop out, but be careful and examine each mushroom before you drop it into the sack.

   I have noted an exception in southern states along rivers and low
areas where some dirt from rain or groundwater swells had risen
into the hollow of a morel stem. Rare, but true.

**Q: We always freeze-dry our morels. Is this the best way to keep
them?**

A: No. Fresh morels have moisture content of over 90%. When
dehydrated by most methods (sun and air screen drying, electric
dehydrator, etc.) the moisture content can only be reduced to 8-
10%. This lies within the acceptable standards for dehydrated product in the United States. There is still water in that mushroom.
The water will freeze in your freezer compartment and melt (deteriorate) when it's thawed. I suggest putting dried morels in a paper
sack and keeping the dry. Big commercial dehydrators can do a
better job of removing moisture. The big mushroom distributors
then often use heavy plastic bags to store the product in, but even
in these situations I've seen spoilage and bugs. The condition of
morels when they're picked is very important in successful preservation. Choose only young, healthy, whole specimens. Older or
damp mushrooms will tend to have more insects, mold and bacteria. And like the old saying, one bad morel can spoil the bunch.

Questions and Answers continue on page 51....................

Verpa Bohemica   SKIRT-CAP MOREL

FALSE

GOOD, but...

DETAILS: 2"- 8" tall, yellow or tan in color, stem yellow or creamy. Appears early in morel season, usually after black morels have stated, in forests. The cap hangs over the stem like a bell or a skirt--stem goes all the way to the inside top of the cap. Stem is filled with a cottony substance (not hollow). Wrinkled cap or smooth. Also known as "conica". Very high moisture content. Hard to preserve. Meaty flavor.

Note "cotton" inside stem, and how cap "sets" on top on stem. Also wrinkles, not pits (sometimes smooth).

Verpa Bohemica   SKIRT-CAP MOREL

FALSE

GOOD, but...

OK to eat if specimens are fresh and healthy. High moisture content conducive to rapid deterioration, mold and bacteria. Keep separate from true morels in collection as contact can spread dampness. Can have a slight muscle relaxant effect, particularly if this species only is eaten. Recommended to mix with true morels in cooking. The only false morel OK to eat, but with caution.

Gyromitra Esculenta   **BEEFSTEAK MOREL**

FALSE
BAD

DETAILS: Liver or tan color, various shapes and sizes, wavy indented caps, cap hangs over stem, stem usually filled with a cotton-like substance. Stem normally convoluted and thick. Found in forests, pines, fields when black morels are "out". Also known as "brains", "globs" or "redheads". Several varieties. Similar to the "saddle morel" (Helvella) in appearance. Not recommended to eat. There have been deaths linked to ingestion of this type.

Gyromitra Esculenta   **BEEFSTEAK MOREL**

FALSE
BAD

Many people have eaten "beefsteaks" for years with no problems, and some claim they're their favorite type of morel. The flavor is meaty. They tend to have more insects in them because of the loose cap and convolutions, and saltwater soaking is recommended if one insists on consuming these. Tip: leave your pot or pan lid off when cooking to allow steam (and toxin) to exit, making them safer to eat.

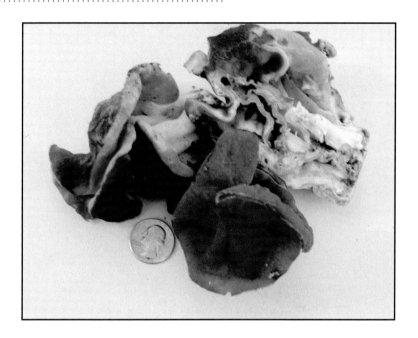

Helvella   **SADDLE MOREL**

FALSE

BAD

This cross-section clearly shows the convoluted texture of the stem and cap of this false morel, as well as the "cotton" in the stem. Note the loose, hanging cap. The Helvella family is tan or reddish in color and usually displays some type of "saddle" shape, i.e. a singular saddle or a small group. The cross-sections of Helvella and Gyromitras are very much alike, with the (normally) wide, twisted stem, loose cap and thick, solid structure. Not recommended for eating.

Helvella   SADDLE MOREL

FALSE
BAD

There are several names and types of the Helvella and Gyromitra fami-
lies (gigas, rotunda, elata, carolinia, conica, rimosipes, infula, etc.), but
they have similar basic characteristics. Some are said to be perfectly
safe to eat. Some certainly aren't safe. All edible and choice mushrooms
should be eaten with caution in all cases.

A beautiful bouquet of fresh, healthy white morels. The white morels will tend to "cluster" more so than the black or giant morels. I once found 23 in one group, growing from one "stem".

Adder's Tongue
or
Trout Lily

Violet

Black morels are not commonly found in clusters. The are predominantly hardy individualists, but morels are wonderfully unpredictable.

Q: Can morels be grown?

A: Yes. Several companies have had success, but only on a limited basis: Neogen Corporation (Lansing, Michigan) and Kuhn Champignon (Herisau, Switzerland) in laboratory settings; Morel Mountain (Mason, Michigan), Mr. Mushroom (Hardeeville, South Carolina) and Terry Farms (Auburn, Alabama) with commercial endeavors. No one to my knowledge has produced a predictably top quality morel in large, regular quantities (my standard being 2000 pounds per week that smell and taste like a Michigan black morel).

Q: Michigan has 4 or 5 morel mushroom festivals. Is Michigan the best place for morels?

A: Michigan may do the best job of promoting their mushroom festivals, along with their large public forests and other attractions. Well over 500,000 people hunt morels every year in the state of Michigan. Morels do grow in every US state, every province of Canada, and even in Mexico. The commercial harvest from the Pacific Northwest reaches levels of over one and one-half million pounds of morels. Forests, particularly hardwoods, and no people is a good combination to start with.

Q: When I re-hydrate morels I use hot water. The water turns brown and is great for soups and gravy. Is this the best method?

A: Hot water probably changes the chemistry of the product a bit, slightly cooking or boiling it. Though this is a popular method because it's fast, dramatic and does add a lot of flavor to the water, I recommend re-hydrating in cool water for 2 hours. It allows the mushrooms to "equilibrate" (a scientific term for reaching their natural state). Though it takes longer the mushrooms will be "fuller" and the water will still have the color and usability. The moisture content roller coaster ride morels take is interesting: 92% water in the woods, dried down to 9%, re-hydrated up to over 80%, then cooked down to 30-40%. Anything that can be done to allow them to fully equilibrate should be a plus.

Q: What's the best way to preserve morels?

A: I've tried everything—freezing, canning and drying—and different methods of each. The half-sauté-then-freeze method is used by the majority of gourmet chefs who buy morels fresh in season and want to extend their availability on their menus. There seems to be a shelf-life factor that could be a concern, though for most they don't last long enough to have to deal with it. It does take some effort and equipment (a freezer, for example). Any time you have to have a perfect "seal", such as in canning or freezing, a problem could occur.

My favorite preservation method is still sun-and-air drying, on a nylon screen. It's quick, easy and usually does not encounter shelf-life problems. I've served 3-year old re-hydrated morels that were every bit as good as month-old ones. I put my whole, un-washed, young healthy specimens on a screen in the sun, raised

Rose Hips

for air circulation. I set it up early in the day and within 8-10 hours they're crisp and ready to store. I store mine in paper bags. I fold the open end over and close with tape. The paper seems to allow the mushrooms to breathe. Plastic tends to trap moisture and build heat.

Q: Morels sure can get mushy fast, especially on a hot day. Why?

A: Most people that make this comment are using plastic bags for collection (bread bags are "big" in the South). Use a breathable mesh bag, please. It's better for you mushrooms and for the environment because it allows spores to drop back to the forest floor where they were intended to go. The other factors in "mushiness" may come from age or moisture on the mushroom after it's up. The moisture could be from moisture, dew or frost. Dampened mushrooms are not good candidates for preservation, especially drying. Be careful not to mix damp or older mushrooms with younger solid specimens as the deterioration can spread.

Q: What's the best way to transport fresh morels?

A: When travelling by auto I recommend using coolers with ice in sealed bags to cool the product. Ice directly on the mushrooms can melt and cause deterioration and have an impact on shelf life and preservability. Try to shade during transport if possible. A car trunk exposed to sunshine can heat up considerably. If this cannot be avoided, do not cover cooler to allow air circulation. If you're going to dry them at your destination, leave them (small amounts, obviously) on the dashboard in a tray or box to start the process.

Q: We used to find tons of morels, but not so anymore. Why?

A: It is entirely possible that the recollection of past harvests has become foggy in the minds of many a morel aficionado, much like fish stories…. That aside, you're quite correct in your observation. The numbers of morels has dropped where they had been more prolific in the past. Increased pesticide use and deforestation has hurt production, but the growing masses of pickers that use paper bags, plastic bags and buckets have seriously reduced the number of spores returning to the land. Considering the fact that it takes years for the spores to produce another mushroom, we can expect more decreased yields. If pickers don't use mesh bags now the trend will continue. Mesh bags should be mandatory.

Q: Can I find morels near my home or do I have to travel to remote areas?

A: You can dramatically increase your chances of finding morels close to home in two ways, both of which are good practice anyway.

1) You can seed areas that look like they might have morels if the spore would just get there. Take fresh morels picked in another location and walk through your selected woods with the morels in a mesh bag. Gently raise and lower the bottom of the bag. Thousands of spores will fall.

2) It's possible that areas near you already have morels—you're just not finding them—yet. Get a notebook. While it's still cold, go on a "scouting drive" and pick out 6-10 spots that might produce morels. Write down the selections and maps to them. They can be relatively close.

The key now is to frequent the spots. If morels normally appear in your area May 1, visit your spots April 15. Go every 3 or 4 days, after work or on weekends, but go regularly. Hit at least 5 spots every time out, but don't spend more that 5 minutes at each. If mushrooms are there you'll see them. On one of your trips you're likely to find something. This tells you the secret—when morels are out in your area this year. Once you know when, then you can hit all the other spots (and more) over the next couple of days (I recommend calling in sick). You will accumulate a list of good producing locations that you can continue to refine. Eliminate the non-producers. Eventually you will have a list of productive spots not far away. You'll still have to frequent the spots to find the "when" factor each year, but you've got a good start.

Jack-in-the-Pulpit

Q: Where'd you find that 80 pounds?

A: I will tell you it happened in mid-Michigan in 1983. The spot has never hit like that again (for me, anyway). The circumstances were, as usual with mushroom hunting, odd. A friend and I had walked nearly two miles, finding only two mushrooms (a mile a mushroom is not a good ratio) and were ready to turn back when we saw a series of "fingers" of land that seemed to extend down and away. Big fat yellow morels, 6-8 inches tall were at the side of an old logging trail that ran between two of the fingers. In that little valley we quickly filled 3 grocery bags. The morels were close enough that we were on hands and knees, and covered the valley that way. I took off my jacket and piled morels on it so we could re-use the bags. We picked slowly up a ridge. At the top was another valley—with golden globes spotted throughout. We looked at each

other and went to work. There were 4 valleys like that. We didn't
get off our hands and knees for 3 ½ hours! The bags were full.
Both jackets were covered. Robyn stayed with the mushrooms
while I made two trips to the car and back. We dried them on
screens the next day and filled 10 grocery bags full with dried morels. We had picked over 80 pounds from that spot. (It's west of
Gaylord, Michigan, off Highway 32).

Q: Which tastes better, black morels or white morels?

A: My standard answer is "I don't care as long as it's a morel," but the
real answer is not that simple. Some chefs have told me emphati-
cally that whites are better. Others just as strongly cite blacks as
superior. My real personal favorite is a deep hardwood forest black
morel. They are very hardy because they're the first type to appear
and survive more hostile conditions. The moisture content is a
little lower than the subsequent white and giant family members,
and I believe the earthy flavor and aroma are a little stronger. The
smell of a fresh black morel in the woods is my favorite outdoor
scent.
           White and giant morels appear after the blacks and are associ-
ated with slightly higher temperatures and more humidity. They're
usually larger with a higher moisture content. They can, conse-
quently, have a shorter life span and deteriorate or dry out more
quickly. The smell is normally not as strong as that of the black
morel. Interestingly, the smell of dried black morels stays earthy
while the smell of whites takes on a hint of maple and walnut.
           I soak all the varieties in cool water for a half-hour to balance
the moisture content before cooking with them. Though I may like
the aroma of the black morel the best, the flavor of all types are in
the same category—delicious!

Q: **How long does it take for spore to become another mushroom?**

A: This is the question that mycologists have been struggling with for decades. It seems that all mushrooms have different life cycles and can take various numbers of generations to mature to a fruiting stage.

   The thinking on morels has been that it tales up to ten years for the entire organism to grow to the point that it bears fruit each season. Recent studies indicate that a specific types of mushroom takes a specific number of generations before they fruit. Some mushrooms take 5 years. One studied took 26 years. Morels seem to take 5 years, so if you have good luck in a spot in the year 2000, mark your calendar to return to that spot in 2005. Bad yields would also be reflected 5 years later.

   Conditions, of course, have a strong influence also. Warm rain followed by cool, dry days and nights will maximize, preserve and prolong the crop. Extended rains (that can dissipate mushrooms in

Dutchman's Breeches

the rain), frosts and freezes, droughts and heat waves all can have adverse effects. And remember, those effects are felt years down the road. I've kept diaries of all my spots for over 25 years and have seen some interesting patterns, which have, in some cases, enabled me to accurately predict results. (Spring of the year 2000 looks to be a good year.)

Dandelion

Q: **I just can't seem to see the darned things. What am I doing wrong?**

A: You're probably not seeing them because they're not there. Many people look when and where they think is right, but for various reasons don't find anything. If you're not seeing any, change locations. Keep moving. Here's some other tips:

     1) Look 10-20 feet away, not directly down, and look for that "Christmas tree" shape (particularly with black morels).

Continued on page 67.......................

....

   Very little in the way of equipment is needed or morel (or other) mushroom hunting, one of the benefits of the "sport". Long pants and long-sleeved shirts are a must, even though the weather may be suitable for walking shorts. Quite often you'll find yourself in areas where the briars and bushes will be unfriendly. I've been in some locations (I won't specifically mention the golf course in Illinois) where the multiflora rose was so thick and hostile that it threatened to shred your clothes while nearly preventing movement at all! Wild berry bushes and nettles can be plentiful. The searching for mushrooms is generally quite pleasant and without difficulty, but it is always wise to be prepared .

   "Comfortable" is the key for walking shoes. Boots are a good choice because of the additional protection afforded.
The areas you will be exploring will dictate the type of shoe you should choose.

   A cap is usually a good idea also. There are spider webs and

twigs and branches that can be bothersome. Hats are good protectors from sun and rain.

I recommend a compass (and knowledge of how to use one. It's not difficult to learn) and a whistle. The compass can help you prevent getting lost or finding a path if you do get lost. The whistle is good to keep track of your group members. Always have whistles for children.

Get a mesh bag and you're ready to go!

The famous "Mushroom walk"-- the long, low stride mushroomers use to move quickly, yet alertly through fields and woods. If you're not finding mushrooms in an area, no matter how promising it looks, keep moving. The low profile of "the walk" is maintained to more advantageously see the outline of a morel cap against the background. Eyes should be focused 10 to 15 feet ahead. Sometimes compared to the Groucho Marx walk.

Late Nite Mushrooming
Top 10 Lies Told By Mushroom Hunters....

10. *They taste terrible. It's the fried butter I like.*

9. *Yes, as a matter of fact, I do own this property.*

8. *No, I'm not mushroom hunting. I love crawling through briar patches.*

7. *I don't know any good spots. Let's check yours.*

6. *Sure, I'll tell you where I found 'em.*

5. *No. I didn't find any.*

4. *Of course I have permission to hunt here.*

3. *It's too early for morels.*

2. *I think those are poisonous--better give them to me for proper disposal.*

1. *The biggest mushroom I ever found had a shadow that weighed 3 pounds.*

The "Top 10" list above available on T-shirts, just one of the fun mushroom items available from Morel Mania. Call (1-800-438-4213), or email: morel@ocslink.com for a complete catalog of carved walking sticks, books, posters, decoys & more. (That's Tom Nauman, the owner).

This photo shows author Lonik with 229 morels he picked in 3 1/2 hours at the Trail of Tears Lodge and Resort in Jonesboro, (southern) Illinois. The interesting fact is that two days prior there was a mushroom festival at Trail of Tears and 134 contestants in the mushroom picking contest gathered a total of over 5000 mushrooms in one day. Lonik picked in the exact same area. Any of several conclusions could be drawn: Lonik's good. He got lucky. The other hunters just plain missed a bunch. More grew in a day and a half. Plus, Lonik had never hunted in the area before. Morels can be found in new places. Be persistent. Don't give up.

Those are morels drying on the screen in the background.

Lonik was so impressed with the Lodge and the area ("There's a lot of land and a lot of mushrooms. I'll be back"), the Lodge owners and he created "Morel Heaven" weekend morel outings, in April, complete with seminars, guided hunts and cooking demonstrations.

More info about these weekends at **www.morelheaven.com**

Mushrom clubs are a wonderful way to learn more about mushrooms and make new friends. Over 100 organizations exist in North America and they meet for forays several times a year and also participate in fairs, dinners and seminars. They usually bring along a mycologist who will help identify whatever is found, using spore prints and other methods, but the total experience of the group and their willingness to share their knowledge plus their enthusiasm, encouragement and comradarie are what make these groups so special, for the newcomer and longtimer. Much of our knowledge of mushrooms comes from descendants of Central European nations, and the clubs often reflect that heritage and dedication.

From left to right, Jim Weber, Nancy SmithWeber (mushroom book author), Lonik, Cheryl Skerceny (future mushroom club President), Royal Olsen (former mushroom club President) and Alexander Smith (renown mycologist and mushroom field guide author). All gathered as part of a Fall mushroom exposition and foray. Club activities usually include experts willing to share their knowledge and experience.

In addition to the remarkable wildflowers and blossoms that populate the forested Spring world, many newly-born animals can occasionally be seen, some truly beautiful and delicate visions, such as the baby horned owl (above) and the fawn (below).

The horned owl was about 6 weeks old, though its wingspan was close to six feet. Its wings were not developed sufficiently to fly completely on its own. It evidently had fallen from its nest to the leaf-covered forest floor where it attempted several times in my presence to fly back to its nest. It would whip up a small tornado of dry leaves as it beat its wings during its takeoff attempt, gradually ramping up, but not strong enough or high enough to reach its destination, and would come crashing awkwardly back down, only to rev up again for more attempts. It finally was exhausted and crouched, "clicking" at me with its already powerful beak to warn me of that I should leave it alone. Of course you should not touch or feed or play with any wild animal, and I didn't.

The fawn was a twin. I came upon both fawns, on opposite sides of a hill, while mushrooming. I usually bring a camera and was fortunate to get this picture and encounter another example of the amazing beauty of Mother Nature.

Still one of the most magnificent photos of morels in the wild, incorporating the leaves, green emerging, trillium and wild violets with a grouping of healthy new white morels. The "photo op" wouldn't have lasted long (short lifespan of morel fruiting bodies), making these scenes rare and special--part of the mystique of the whole experience.

(Questions and answers continued from page 58)

I'm 6 foot 7 so I scan even farther away and have spotted morels at distances of 50 feet. 45 years of experience helps too.

Children often make good mushroom hunters because they're lower to the ground (and have better eyesight and more energy) and notice the shapes. I use the famous Groucho Marx-like "mushroom walk" to lower my eye level. Also, after 45 years of practice, I've turned into a "Morel Terminator". My eyes find the shapes I'm seeking then scan the shapes for the desired sponge-like texture. I'll walk at a fast pace through a woods and only stop when I'm alerted to a visual shape/texture positive match. I can check a woods quickly to determine if I should move to another spot or not. Maybe one spot was good yesterday or will be good tomorrow. I'm always on the move until I find a morel.

2) Frequent spots. If you found morels in one area last May 22, they could be 3 weeks earlier this year, or 3 weeks later. Start looking early in the season and be persistent.

3) Bring along a picture. If you look for hours and don't find any morels your eyes can get tired. Remind them of the target.

Q: Can dogs be trained to find morels, like pigs for truffles?

A: Truffles and morels are in the same genetic family-- ascomycetes. They reproduce from sac-like spore and store nutrients in an underground warehouse called sclerotia. Truffles absorb moisture over several months, then expand and crack the soil around the fruiting body. New spore is released from the crack. The aroma at that time is like an entire spice cabinet dumped—most living beings could detect it. The use of pigs enhances the romantic myth as much as it is practical, but, yes, pigs can be trained to smell truffles. Dogs are used to locate them also.

Dogs can be trained to find morels, though I know of only three examples. One man trained a young beagle pup to point at a morel. The dog was hit by a car and killed, but the man then trained a mutt that would stand over a morel.

My dog, Crimson, I believe was the smartest morel hunting dog ever (and he wouldn't argue with that). A golden retriever-Irish setter mix, Crimson always knew he was smarter than I was. In the woods he would always lead the way and, over the years, would begin to make decisions on where to go in certain situations. For example, he would come to a clearing with pines on one side, rolling wooded hills on another and a field in front. He'd look around and go toward the rolling hills. 50 feet behind, I'd come to the same spot, look around, and as I started toward the hills, see Crimson ahead, looking back to make sure I got it right. His selections were nearly always what I'd do. Later he figured out what I was looking for and would bark and point when he found a morel. We hunted together for 12 years. I told this story to a group of people I was taking on a guided mushroom hunt. We parked all the cars, synchronized watches, established a return time and directions, and I said, "Let's go!" Crimson took off into the woods, leading the way as usual, and the entire group ran after him! I could hear "Where's the red dog" and "Follow the red dog" as I was left alone, yelling to the disappearing group, "*I'm* the expert! *I'm* the author! *I'm* the guide! Isn't anybody going to follow *me*?"

Eventually Crimson decided he'd taught me all he could, which I think is a lot.

Mayapple

I am always looking for more information (unusual experiences, recipes, mushroom- and nature-related activities, photos, drawings, picking times in all areas, hot spots, tall tales, etc.). Please write or email me c/o the publisher....

RKT Publishing   PO Box 182   Hazel Park,   MI 48030

Email: **TREE@www.morelheaven.com**

web: **www.morelheaven.com**

Check out the website for personal appearance schedules, photos, new stuff and more mushroom fun.

Best wishes and good hunting always!

"Tree"

MORE FUN WITH NATURE AND COOKING

BASICALLY MORELS : MUSHROOM HUNTING, COOK-ING, LORE & ADVICE (Larry Lonik). The book that started it all--now updated and revised from cover to cover. The whos, whats, wheres, whens, whys and hows of successful morel hunting and cooking (60 recipes--from campfire basics to gourmet kitchen). Preservation tips, mushroom clubs, festivals & much more. The first and most popular book of its kind, and easily the most fun – now even better! 144 pages. 6 X 9. B/W photos, illustrations. *$11.95.*

MORELS & MORE: WILD MUSHROOMS AND GOUR-MET RECIPES, TALES & TIPS (Larry Lonik). Morel, bolete, chanterelle, shiitake, portabello, matsutake, oyster, truffle, black trumpet, enoki, porcini and maitake – wonderful mushrooms that one can find in the forests and at specialty suppliers. Fabu-lous gourmet recipes (60). Inside "scoops" on where and when to find these mushrooms, mushroom cultivation , mushroom hunting tips, humorous stories and more. 160 pages. 6 X 9. 32 pages of beautiful full COLOR photos. B/W photos, illustra-tions. *$14.95.*

MORELS: TRUE OR FALSE: THE ESSENTIAL FIELD GUIDE & MORE (Larry Lonik). Finally, an easy-to-use, up-to-date Field Guide that clearly shows the good and the bad, and how to tell them apart. Full COLOR photos of the seven most common "morels" one can encounter in the Spring – in their natu-ral habitat and cross-sectioned. The latest and most accurate in-formation -- from the World's No. 1 morel expert! With all the widespread (surely unintentional) bad info out there, an absolute MUST. Plus a unique question/answer section that will make your mushroom experiences safer and more productive, whether you're a novice or a seasoned pro. 80 pages. 6 X 9. 32 pages of COLOR photos B/W photos, illustrations. *$11.95*

THE HEALTHY TASTE OF HONEY: BEE PEOPLE'S RECIPES, ANECDOTES & LORE (Larry Lonik). Amazing facts about bees, honey, pollen, beeswax, beekeeping, history, medicine, health, and humor.... Plus over 150 delicious recipes in a variety of categories. Did you know when they dug up King Tut's tomb they found honey that was still edible? Learn and enjoy. Bee healthy! 170 pages. 6 X 9. B/W photos, illustrations. *$11.95.*

MOREL MUSHROOM HUNTING VIDEO. COLOR 60 minutes. As seen on PBS. Everything you ever wanted to know, see or hear about morels. *$19.95.*

MOREL COOKING VIDEO. COLOR. 60 minutes. From the campsite to the gourmet kitchen. Basic all-time favorites plus a taste of the exotic. Special guest, internationally-heralded chef Tom MacKinnon. Seen on PBS. *$19.95.*

TO ORDER:
AUTOGRAPHED BOOKS & VIDEOS
By mail: Send check or money order to
  RKT PUBLISHING
  PO Box 182
  Hazel Park, MI 48030
Include a list of items you want, who you want them (it) autographed to and your return address. Add a $4.00 flat shipping & handling fee for any size order.
Or order from our website:

www.morelheaven.com

(The RKT TOLL FREE order number is listed on the website)

Or order from BOOKWORLD 1-800-444-2524
        or MOREL MANIA 1-800-438-4213

ABOUT THE AUTHOR

Naturalist Larry Lonik is a man of many interests. He has been successful in the business world, draws and paints, composes and performs music and has created for educational television and motion pictures. BASICALLY MORELS is Larry's fifth book in his Nature/ Cooking series, which began with THE HEALTHY TASTE OF HONEY, first published in 1981.

He has produced videos on Mushroom Hunting and Cooking that have aired on PBS. He's appeared on CNN, National Public Radio, many TV and radio shows, been active with seminars, guided mushroom hunts and cooking demonstrations. He was a primary player at Morel Mountain and Mr. Mushroom, two breakthrough companies that grew morels commercially. He's currently doing research with mushrooms for arthritis and cancer.

Larry is fascinated with the application of scientific principles to Man and his environment. "The answers are right in front of us — what we are, where we came from... how to be productive, efficient, effective, healthy and happy." The 6-foot 7-inch native of Michigan (nicknamed "Tree") and graduate of Michigan State University combined 25 years of research (personal study, interviews with botanists, mycologists, chefs, public officials and countless morel enthusiasts) with 45 years of personal mushroom picking, eating and growing experience to produce the latest trio of BASICALLY MORELS, MORELS & MORE and MORELS: TRUE OR FALSE.